CERTAIN PATTERNS

HASTINGS WYMAN, JR

WPH
Washington Writers'
Publishing House

Some of these poems have appeared in the following publications: *Aura, Cedar Rock, Rustlings, Southern Poetry Review, Sun, Three Sisters, Tinderbox, Washington Review of the Arts, The Washingtonian* and in the anthologies, *The Poet Upstairs* and *The Other Side of the Hill*.

© 1982, Hastings Wyman, Jr.   All rights reserved
Printed in the United States of America   First Edition

Typography by Kathryn E. King

The publication of this book has been made possible in part by a grant from the Hechinger Foundation, Time-Life Books of Alexandria, and the services donated by many friends.

ISBN Number 0-931846-22-6
Library of Congress Card Number 81-86641

Photo by William Hennefrund

Washington Writers' Publishing House
P.O. Box 50068
Washington, DC 20004

For my father,
who told me stories,
and my mother,
who sang me songs.

CONTENTS

SOUTHERN POEMS
- Aunt Anna — 7
- Lending A Hand With The Laundry — 8
- Spree — 10
- Surgery — 11
- The Lynching — 13
- Mistletoe — 16
- End of Summer — 17
- Daddy Talks About The New House — 18
- Rising Behind — 20
- Soup Kitchen — 21
- Down Home — 22
- I Watch — 25

CHURCH POEMS
- The Priest — 27
- The Vestry — 28
- Seminarians — 29
- The Rector's Wife — 30
- Wallington Hopkins — 31
- Annie Bloodworth — 32
- With Timbrel and Dance — 33
- Reception — 34
- Bazaar — 35
- Christmas Eve — 36

WORK POEMS
- Puzzle — 37
- To Our Speedreading Teacher — 38
- Report On The Sick — 39

DREAM POEMS
- Some Ruse — 41
- I Hit A Bearded Man — 42
- Certain Patterns — 44
- December Trips and Dreams — 46

OTHER POEMS
- Repairs — 49
- Navigating — 50
- Waiting For Tuesday — 51
- Diet — 52
- Hats — 53
- The New Year — 54

SOUTHERN POEMS

AUNT ANNA

Aunt Anna talked
about the Yankee
soldiers, how they

poured the rice
and molasses
in the dirt,

how her grand-
mama picked
the grains from

the gooey ground
to feed the
family. When

Aunt Anna
left the room,
I tried the

piano. It was
soundless. "They
must have stolen

the piano wires,
too," my uncle
said. We laughed

as Aunt Anna
returned, face
stern, to serve

supper.

LENDING A HAND WITH THE LAUNDRY

Whenever Aunt Anna
went to the country
to get the laundry
she took the boys with her
to carry it to the car.

They drove out in the county
past where the paved roads stop
to a poor washwoman's
poor unpainted house.

The laundry lay loose
in a large wicker basket
out on the front porch,
smelling like lye,
like the hot black pot
on the backyard fire.

Daddy and his brother
both said that those
were the heaviest
dry clothes
they ever lifted,
struggled, strained
with all their might
to carry in the dark of night
to their Hudson Terraplane.

They carefully settled
their heavy burden,
this lead-like laundry,
into the trunk.

Aunt Anna's
deft hands
tucked underwear under
each round glass container
carefully cushioning
the bottles and jars
of illegal booze
for the long journey back
over rough
washboard
roads.

SPREE

It was twenty thousand
by one account, forty
by another. But when
Uncle Dave's dad died,
he and Aunt Anna took
off for the city to
spend. They leased
a suite in the Jefferson
for six months, drank
till they ran out of
friends, then to Atlanta
for six more. Anna
danced naked on tables.
Once they found Dave
propped up plastered
in bed in Anna's gown.
When a year and the
money were gone, they
came back to town.
Dave became main-
tenance man at
the library, swept
hard marble floors,
remembered carpeted
halls. Neither he
nor Anna ever looked
sad after that. He
died an Elder in the
Church, she later
quietly.

SURGERY

Daddy talked about the
carnival that came to the county.
Lots of strange foreign people.
Gypsies and the like
that did other-worldly
things.

One show featured a highly
skilled daredevil
who rode a motorcycle
at high speed
around and around
a large wooden bowl,
like half a giant barrel,
until the centrifugal force
held him horizontal
to the ground.

One of the farmers
whether mesmerized,
forgot what he was doing,
what he was chewing,
or just out of spite
spit
tobacco juice
on the slick wooden wall.
The motorcycle flew out of control.
Cycle and cyclist
skidded, slid and smashed
to frantic disaster,
scaring and scattering
the fascinated, frightened farmers.

Leaving a battered
machine and a mangled
man with alien eyes
who cried in pain
begging for God and a
bunch of weird saints
to save his soul and
his leg.

His leg was what Daddy knew about.
His leg and a lot of whiskey
to absorb the agony
while Daddy's daddy
doctored, with uncertain sight
and poor light
in the Operating Room
on the first floor of their home.

The leg was lost.
And Daddy,
a wide-eyed youth
with good hands,
tied off the arteries
from the severed limb.

The gypsy recovered and
rejoined the carnival,
but doing what
Daddy didn't
know.

THE LYNCHING

In the 'twenties they roared
in small towns too. Daddy
was in his 'teens, and he
told me everybody was
talking about it,
up in arms about it.

The Sheriff and his
men went to a house
because of some trouble
between two colored men
and one colored woman.
One of 'em stuck a shotgun
out the window and
shot the Sheriff dead.
He never had a chance.

They had all three in
jail. Trouble was,
nobody knew who actually
fired the gun. Was it
the tall black man?
Or the woman's slender hand?
Who knew?

Daddy climbed up in a tree
like Zacheus to listen
to the Sheriff's Deputy
tell a mob of low class
trash to go home and
let the law do its job.
The mob broke up

muttering. That night
persons unknown broke
into the jail.
Took all three,
took the female
with the men.

Once in fear the three
broke loose, ran in
the Catholic Church.

But that was no sanctuary
to hardened Calvinists suspicious
of everything outside
the poor white part of town
near the cotton mill.
Anyway, they didn't
come to pray,
they came to kill.

Daddy was in bed,
heard his daddy's phone
ring. Then his daddy
said, "Get up, get up!
We have to go. The
voice on the phone was
one I don't know. And
he didn't want a pill.
All he said was, 'Doc,
there's three dead niggers
on Crosland Hill.' "

Daddy and his daddy went,
found three bodies—
two men,
one woman,
three lengths of rope
tightly wound round
three black necks.

Daddy said it was a shame.
Said the white trash had to blame
somebody and they got one
right for sure,
besides two who
didn't do it.

Years later some yankee wrote a book—
said the Sheriff's wounds were in his back,
said some white deputy must've done it,
that not one of the three blacks was in it.

We never believed that for a minute.

MISTLETOE

In 1910 at age 16
my grandmother
left the train
midway from New York
to Texas. At 18
she married a
doctor twice her
age, bore four
children.

The Depression hit.
She ran out on her
husband and the
whole damn town.
If I ever come
back, she said,
I'll walk down
Main Street with
mistletoe tied up
above my ass.

Nothing worked the
way she wanted:
The man who sold
gold stocks was
a fraud; the rare
book dealer a
thief.

She later made a
living selling
houses. Even
after her stroke,
she kept her hair
cut short, smoked
and wore slacks.

Visiting a son's
grave, she read
familiar stones. If
all of them can stand
it I can too, she
said.

Her three children
—one a doctor,
another a nurse—
by her side,
she died.

END OF SUMMER

They packed up
and tanked up
wound round
and down
the mountain
turned around
to count kids
found they had
left all three
at the top   swore
off for two weeks

DADDY TALKS ABOUT THE NEW HOUSE

The house has lots
of what your
Mama calls motors
    pumping heat
    cooling air
    washing and
    drying dishes
    and clothes
    grinding garbage
    packing trash
And a ring that turns
hot and burns impurities
from the air.

I figured out a new
hearing aid gizmo to
help me hear half
again as well.
At the Elders'
meeting the church
air conditioner
whines out what
people are saying;
I ask questions
that have been
covered.

Built the house
myself to sell,
moved in instead.
It's built tight
cheap to heat
close three doors
use three rooms
open up the rest
when you children
come home to
stay upstairs
with your kids
we can all
have our privacy.

Soon I'm eligible
for Social Security.
The Savings and Loan
gives me a good
net worth and I've
got money in the
savings account and the
business account and the
Kehoe account and
Certificates of Deposit.

The carpet is not
the only thing
soft around here;
Those blood pressure
pills kill me
deader than a doornail.

The house is
all paid for.
Ought to sell
fast for a
good price.

I've got to
decide too about
running again
for City Council;
your Mama don't
much want me to.
    (I don't want
      anybody saying
    he's too old).

And I don't owe
a damn dime.

That's not bad for
someone that had
to borrow money
to move down here,

And putting you
children through
school,

Not bad.

RISING BEHIND

We planned a
barbecue to
help put Barry
in the White House,

bought a pig,
took it to a
black man in the
country to cook

meat, hash and
sauce. His plump
brown daughter
leaned over an

oak chip fire
stirring, her skirt
rising behind.

I stared, caught
her father's eye,
turned pink.
"Republicans,

huh?" he asked.
I nodded. "Hope
it kill forty
of you," he said.

SOUP KITCHEN

A one-eye-
running, one-
legged black
beggar called
Rooster stood
looking into
my two blue
eyes, smelled
fear, sneered,
made me feel
inferior.

DOWN HOME

We take the back-
road, notice
four layers of
color: the ground
is the grayish
brown of dead
grass; then a
layer of dark
brown leaves
still on the
scrub oaks;
above them, deep
green of taller
pines, then
bright blue sky.
Mary says she's
always liked
pine green against
blue sky.

We drive out
to the Springfield
fork, take a right
on the State Park
road, then another
right that becomes
two ruts through
scrub oaks and
pines and
finally we
come to the
cabin by the
pond to the
party. The
men have been
hunting ("Shooting
shit birds," one
says, "little
blackbirds that
shit.") but
they talk about
other things—

    I'm growing corn,
Tom says, and
soybeans—
no cotton. We
always planted at
least five or six
hundred acres of
cotton, but not
any more. Now
it's corn and
soybeans and a
little wheat (not
much wheat—you
could have crop
failure all over
the southeast,
and the midwest
could still
glut the wheat
market.) I'm
holding my
corn and soy-
beans off the
market, hoping
the price will
rise. Fertilizer
is double what it
was last year—
and I bought it
from a friend;
he shaved the
price as much
as he could.

    Remember, Sarah
says, when we
were at the

beach and I
was pregnant?
And Sue and
Janet were
too, all of
us big as
barns? We
all went out
and partyed
late and I
woke up early
and had to
pee. Everybody
else was sound
asleep. I waited
as long as I
could, then I
just couldn't
hold it anymore.
I had to
go through
two rooms of
men to get
to the bath-
room. In the
first room, I
saw Jim's
thing sticking
straight up
and in the
second, your
bare ass was
hanging out.
I laughed, and
after I peed,
I went and
got Sue to
see too.

Alan says:
I said, 'Howard,
how about a favor?

I need another year
on that note I owe.'
Howard said, 'Fine.'
When I got
the note in
the mail, sure
enough, I had
a year's extension.
But the interest
rate had gone
from nine percent
to twelve.

Howard grins.

They all love
each other, we
say. If you told
them they love
each other,
they'd think
you were crazy.
But it's true,
they love
each other.

The natural gas
pumping station
has bright blue
pipes, as blue
as the sea, sky
blue, eye-blue,
expensive wooden
toy blue. The
blue pipes are
large—two
arms in a circle's
worth. They
curve and connect.
They are set off
against a large
silver shed, the

entire complex
chain-link fenced
and nestled in
red clay and
pines by a
newly paved road.
I like the
natural gas
pumping station.

A tree against
the sky is
gray-dark shadow,
the sky a cold
and distant
yellow. The
light in the
kitchen is
pale and warm.
How good
and lonely I
feel. I want
to cry.

I WATCH

I watch my
father and my
son together.

They tease
back and forth
and laugh. My

father is gentler
than I remember,
my son tougher

than I remember
being. I see
myself in each.

It pleases me.

CHURCH POEMS

THE PRIEST

A shaman presiding over the magic
in our lives with vestments, candles
and other anachronistic implementa,
giving form where there is no shape,
reason where there is no sense.

We suspect he's full of bull.
(He suspects he's full of bull.)

We conspire to deny
that God may be a stand-in
for our ignorance, or
worse, dead, meaning
we are all we have.

We demand of our magician
more than he is.
Push him.
Crowd him.

Like Oz's Wizard, he cries
and makes a litany
of God's death:

We are what we are.
Amen.

THE VESTRY

The Vestry—twelve
men and women
good and true—
supervised a cemetery.

The Church and burial
ground fell on hard
times, sold plots
cheap for welfare graves.

In summer when air
is soft there was
no business for the
would-be potter's field.

In winter when the
ground is as hard
as city sidewalks
money rolled in.

The members of
the Vestry made
jokes and
felt bad.

SEMINARIANS

"They come and go,
these young ones do,"
the old lady said.
"And I forget them,

their names and
faces merging
into a picture of
nice young people.

They come for a
year or two, work
their way into
our lives and leave

less fresh,
more seasoned,
I look forward
to the new ones,

but I always miss
them when they go,
our lives blending
into their priesthood."

THE RECTOR'S WIFE

Our living room's
like Grand Central
Station. People
come and go, show
no respect for our
private lives.

On the first floor
there's a door
leading right into
the apse. I need
to let some time
elapse without

having to care for
some stranger or
smile at her child
or bandage a wound
not my own, to be
alone. I need air.

WALLINGTON HOPKINS

On festive occasions
the parish serves
sherry to celebrate
life politely.

Wallington brings
a bottle of bourbon,
stores it by the
punch cups in
the kitchen.

The parish went
caroling with
hot buttered
rum; Wally went
drinking and singing,

later saw
friends pretend
to walk like him,

laugh at his slow
stiff strut.

Cock without a tail.

ANNIE BLOODWORTH

Miss Annie is old,
and living alone,
she always stays
late at church
suppers.

She listens and
giggles and gossips
in whispers, remaining
soft-spoken and
gentle.

On Sunday when they
try something new—
change thou to you
—or spoil the
rhythm,

Mrs. Bloodworth boils
and steams out pouting,
shaking and shouting
causing a one-woman
schism.

WITH TIMBREL AND DANCE

One Palm Sunday several
years ago, a visiting
troupe danced a chancel
drama of The Passion. Brass
rails to the altar were
removed to give them room.

Seven tall young women
dressed in pink and wine
processed to trumpets. Dark
hair pinned up and back,
faces closed to what they
felt, bodies lean and

taut, they leapt and
turned. Long slender
arms made arcs. Hands held
a cross, a sword, a cloak,
a crown of thorns. We
sat in silence, some in tears.

Later an old lady dismissed
as mad by most of us railed
against removal of the
rails: "When they were
installed, in memory of
my mother, workmen talked

about how hard they were
to raise. 'Never take them
down,' they said, 'or you
will never get them back
up right.' " Now on our
way to bread and wine,

we wobble with unstable
rails, remember an old woman's
words, the beauty of the dance.

RECEPTION

At coffee hour, our
cookies crumble into
small black hands that
vanish when tall white
people screech One each!
These apparently parentless
kids intimidate our own.
We call them down.
They call us mother
truckers.

What do we do? Treat
them as our own? Send
them home? Do we turn
our backs on blacks?
Last week they ate Mrs.
Bloodworth's Lady Baltimore
cake. Took her hours to
make.

What do we do? We
make a rule. For Sunday
School parents must sign
kids up. The only thing
to do.

Poor black parents stayed
away. Their kids did
too.

Our Bishop visits. Black
and polished. Lion of
Judah. We cheer. Have
punch and cookies. Chocolate
chip.

BAZAAR

Paint and polish
Cut and sew
Bake, cook and can

Glue jewels
Pot plants
Put up posters

Set up tables
Carry cartons
Unbox books

Sell, hawk
Cut prices
Quit, pack
Sweat

Snap, snarl
Carp

Count cash

CHRISTMAS EVE

Pungent pine and
cedar wreaths
round pillars up-
holding our ceiling.

One hundred candles
glow. We glow. We
are the party after
the party. We're high.

Our choir is higher.
We carol to wind,
string and brass.

We commune, drink
to the life of a
child, smile tears.

Glow into the cold
to a hundred homes.

WORK POEMS

PUZZLE

An executive where
I once worked
pissed daily

in his trash can.
Maids were afraid
they'd be blamed

for his mess, so
for a week after
work, guards

taped his office
shut till his
trash can contents

could be analyzed.
When they had
him cold, they

fired his ass.
We joked about
his pissing

his life away
and wondered
why he did it

this way.

TO OUR SPEED-READING TEACHER

Freud says the
meaning of life
is to work

and to love,
and if you
do one better

the other
improves too.
Free of sub-

vocalization
and limited
vision, we

read fast
and love
slow. Thanks.

REPORT ON THE SICK

I am tired from
a tedious day at
work, but I must
make a speech to
an old men's club
in Sunset Village.

I know I will
hate the place—
and being with a
bunch of old people.
The chairman gives

a report on the
sick: "Jim's too
weak to see his
friends and can't
go out because his
bones are brittle."

"I hear he can't
have sex," says
one old man.
"Well, he can
dream about it,"
says another.

After my speech,
they ask incisive
questions for an
hour. As I ride
home, the moon is
bright and ripe.

DREAM POEMS

SOME RUSE

When I was young
I used to dream
of driving to the coast
to be a star.
The car was always
red, the top down.
Now my sleep unfolds
a red convertible.
I try my key,
try to get away
in time, take
you with me
under some ruse
before they stop us.

I HIT A BEARDED MAN

Lately at night I
hate to go to sleep.
Within minutes, I am
drowning in a pool of

shallow water, my arms
and legs immobilized.
I fight myself awake,
go back to sleep, and

see a man standing
at the foot of my bed.
I scream him away
(he is old), run out

the door (of our house
of twenty years ago)
to curse the men
getting into cars.

I call them pieces of
shit. I throw rocks
and chunks of brick
at them. I hit a

bearded man who
stares in disbelief.
Terror approaches from
another direction. I

scream and throw and
run back in my
house to a woman
(my mother? my wife?)

who welcomes me under
a cloak. There are
children there. It
rains. I run back

to the yard. My
screams are weapons.
They scare me
through the night.

CERTAIN PATTERNS

Certain patterns in my
life are taking shape.
On Russell's day
off, he comes down-
town to lunch. We

go to the same
cafe, flirt with the
folksinger and talk
about the women in our
poetry group. Then

we walk two blocks
to a bookstore, browse,
buy nothing and say
good-bye. On cold days
when I'm alone for

lunch, I buy a half-
smoke sausage from the
vendor on the corner,
eat it while walking
and people-watching.

The sausage is hot,
the air cold, and I
regulate one with the
other. Then I get a
cone of frozen yogurt

for dessert. There
are days when I sit
for hours clipping papers
for my files—or type
up poems and send them

out to publishers, always
adding one new publication.
Sometimes I scrape the
dishes and load the washer,
wrestle with my son or

listen to my daughter
tell about the funny
things at school. When
we have a party, I like
to polish silver, or

cut up vegetables for
the dip. In a dream
I go through a door—
I am the river, the
wind and the sea.

DECEMBER TRIPS AND DREAMS

A sister
and I step
into the
hall, deliver
another sister's
baby. We
take it
to my old
room in
the front of
the house
where I was
always afraid
to sleep.

I went to
Denver,
bought a
leather pouch
of marbles
for my son
and for my
daughter,
a beaded
purse. His
was Made
in Haiti,
hers in
Hong Kong.

We leave
two Jewish
children in
the Arab Zone,
run a risk
to save them.
My cousin
talks about
how much
he has changed.

In Atlantic
City we went
to a ca-
sino. We
walked among
the slot
machines and
black jack
tables. A
well-dressed
young man
smiled at
the noise of
cards and
quarters, his
excitement
showing through
his trousers.

A thin young
man jumps
about. I
draw back
my fist,
miss and
hit the
lamp as
I wake.

I flew to
Houston,
took a
bus to the
Whitehall
Hotel. My
room had a
bath and
a half and
a black book
of matches

with my
name in gold.

We move in-
to the mansion,
complain at
first about
the eggs our
neighbors
toss. Now
the lawn
is thick
and green.
We watch
cars speed
by behind
the fence.

I remember
it wrong
again. I
change the
words and
tone of
voice, adding
menace and
pain where
none was
meant or
felt. Now
my fears
are justi-
fied.

I remember
flirting with
the waitress
at The Bakery
in Chicago,
the smell
of coffee,
the way she
moved her
hands telling
about dessert,
steam on
windows and
a cold night.

For the first
time in thirty-
nine years, I
like my face—
my beard, my
eyes and
the way they
smile. I like
my boots, too,
and my new
down jacket.
Next month
I will be
forty.

OTHER POEMS

REPAIRS

The plumber
fumbling in
the top of
the toilet

doesn't care
about us or
our house. He
leaves loosely

wrenched pipes
which soon leak.
Winter winds
make ice on

the glass and
the glazier
making storm
windows won't

call back. We're
afraid the elec-
trician's lack of
skill will kill

us. The plumber
has Love and
Hate tattooed
on his fingers.

NAVIGATING

We laugh about
the time when
driving drunk

through thick fog
we stopped, opened
the doors and

felt with our
hands to tell
if pavement

or grass was
beneath the car.
Now at night

I dream my
hands are thick,
my legs like

heavy blocks.
And there are
fog-bound days

when I move
robot-like
to each

appointed task.
I can't remember
whether grass

or tar touched
our numb
fingers, only

that we made
it through the
slow night home.

WAITING FOR TUESDAY

> "Everyone has thought of suicide, but then we think, Next Tuesday might be fun."
>
> Stranger on the subway.

Thursday was a
good day, but then
things started down
hill. The brakes on
the car went bad, to the
tune of $140. Then the trans-
mission—another $190—and only
17,000 miles on the mother. I learned
I lost a poetry competition and had to take
the bus to East Jesus during rush hour to pick
up the car. When I got home, I was hungry and angry
—"hangry," my wife said. We went out to my favorite
restaurant. I tried something new. It turned out to be
the meat of internal organs. It tasted like I imagine
dog kidney would taste. I had to eat from the
children's plates. Then over the weekend,
I moved the furniture off the back porch
and got a friend to help me take down
the old wall board. I typed up
poems and sent them out. I
brought my office files up
to date. We went out to
eat again Monday night.
The food wasn't
half-bad.

DIET

I did
not eat
ice cream
today.

HATS

My friend Howard lived in the corner house two blocks
up the street. In his backyard was a pool for gold-
fish. We climbed on the cemented rock fountain in
the center of the pool, and picked lily pads. I picked
one close to the stem and wore it to school as a hat.
A big guy in the second grade tore it up.

In high school, six of us traveled to a nearby town
for a student council conference. Between meetings,
we went into a store that sold hardware and workclothes
and bought green and yellow hats with short bills. The
next day all six of us wore them to school. A guy in
the Senior Class said You think you're a cat, don't
you? I said Well, yeah. He said Let me see you lick
your ass. I quit wearing my hat.

Summer before last I bought a white cloth hat from a
street vendor. It was cheap, and in a few weeks, it
rumpled into something resembling a fishing hat. I
wore it on the way to work to keep the hot sun off my
bald head. People began looking at me like I looked
silly wearing a business suit and a wrinkled hat. I
was glad when the kids lost it playing dress-up out
of doors.

Last Christmas my wife gave me a thick black fur hat.
When my friend Murray saw it, he said Oh, you got a
Russian snatch for Christmas. I laughed. I told my
wife. She laughed. We call it the snussian ratch so
the children won't quote and embarrass us. It keeps
my head warm.

THE NEW YEAR

The year is
new and so
you too do

not remain
unchanged.
Some experience

in love or
war or work
could make

you a little
wiser, the
year ahead a

little better.
So toast the
new year in

knowing this
deadline is
not arbitrary,

but the sun
and moon
conspire to

remind you
that time is
on your side.